A Life Lived Differently

Kathryn Jacobs
and
Rachel Jacobs

Better Than Starbucks
Publications

A Life Lived Differently

First Printing: ISBN 978-1-7376219-4-2

Cover Image: Head of a Boy Singing (1898) drawing by Luc-Olivier Merson

Better Than Starbucks Publications
P.O.Box 673, Mayo, FL 32066

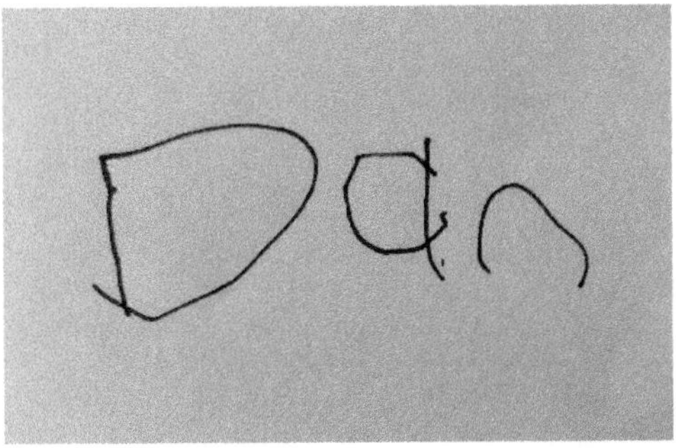
Dan

Kathryn's Prologue — aka Dan the Grown Up

In many ways, *A Life Lived Differently* is about disconnect. Dan has an active mental life but finds himself out of sync with a world he nevertheless does his damndest to make sense of. In this he is aided by his mom, who tries equally hard to craft a workable compromise — and believe me, it ain't easy. Then there's the increasing disconnect between Dan's father and her (because special needs can stress a marriage). Finally there is Joshua, the neuro-typical younger brother who does his best to be helpful — with mixed results. In short, *A Life Lived Differently* is about an American family full of well-meaning people who actually *like* each other — and it's still a struggle. Because life is like that.

Re The Disconnect: Dan just read this and is protesting. Let me make it clear then that Dan himself is not in the *least* confused; on the contrary, it's the *World* that is inconsistent. About pronouns for instance: he wants all of you to understand that "I" and "you" cannot possibly be trusted, because they jump around too much. That's why Dan insists on writing about himself in the third person; "Dan" doesn't change. It's also why he has so much trouble with that trick question, "How are you?" You all say it, but only certain answers are allowed, and he doesn't always know which one.

There, Dan approves now.

Kathryn Jacobs, the poet

Rachel's Prologue: Mom

I expected Dan to learn to talk earlier than he did. I expected Dan to talk more than he did. I expected lots of things that were wrong for Dan. Over the years, I learned how to mother my autistic son, but that wasn't all. Since words were hard for Dan, they were a gift we did not always get. For years the easiest words for him were always about the Wild Kratts. I learned years ago to accept stories about Martin when I asked what had happened at school. At least it was communication. And we knew school was hard. We were proud of Dan for giving so much to school even when it meant he didn't have much left for himself or for us. At first school was so overwhelming that he couldn't eat dinner. We fed him seconds and thirds on the days he could eat. And I learned how to improve my questions about school. Over time I learned to use formulas. I asked about feelings to help him practice and I was happy if he told me about more than the chocolate milk at school. Still, as I watched, I was pretty sure my little boy was happy. His teacher said he had friends. And I knew he was smart even though his teacher said he didn't work hard.

Except he did work hard. I couldn't know what was going on in Dan's head but the screams of anguish when everything was too bright and too loud showed how hard he worked. The frantic jumping on the couch spoke the words Dan couldn't. I knew that when a first grader is constantly off task, they are too young to be the problem. Finally, after great deliberation, we moved Dan to a different school. We worried because we knew Dan liked his teacher and his classmates, particularly N. But we felt young Dan deserved better.

And these last six months, my son has opened up. He tells me long stories now. They're not always responses to the questions asked but that will come. Today, in answer to my question about school, I hear about Giant Martin the Zombie Cat, or was that Kratt. Anyway, Martin stands "like this" (posing rampant with hands like claws) when he sees a scary cat like a lion or a tiger. Other days I hear about playing with R or about recess. And some days I even hear about those precious rare things, feelings. Yesterday out of the blue Dan told me how he enjoyed being friends with R though he missed N from his old school. And when we went to visit family, Dan opened up the way he hasn't in years and told them all about what he was thinking, imagining, and drawing. When his uncle asked questions, Dan incorporated those into the final product. When his uncle pushed, Dan confidently pushed back. Now I know for sure my boy is happy. He says so.

Rachel Jacobs, the prosaist

Table of Contents

Drawing The Pesky Questions

Mom says words itch me, but they're more like bites:
a swarm of stinging questions *chomp* on me,
and Dan has memorized the answers, but
she keeps demanding new ones. There are days
when Dan can almost *see* her questions; when
they squirm like tickly fingers on Dan's skin;
like screams that wiggle. So Dan painted them:

he made his picture full of question marks
and watched them drip; they look like jellyfish,
but Dan pretends they're melting. If he waits
their shoes will be awash with questions, and
then Dan will jump and stomp them back again:
wet, sticky questions in their faces, and

we'll see how much *they* like it —

Dan's Things

I love Dan's art, but I don't understand it. Lots of faces, often angry and surreal scenery, drawn with such precision. He tells the story as he draws, and there's always a lot to learn. But if I miss the telling of the story, then I am left to wonder. So often there is food to cook, dishes to wash, or laundry to fold. But who is that there? And why is he so mad?

I got home late from work this evening. The boys were very glad to see me, but there was even more to do than usual. So when Dan started drawing, I was getting out food for dinner. It tumbled out of the freezer, frozen meat and boxes all over. Dan hated the noise, and I could have done without being hit by the ground beef. The cranberries came out of the package, all over the kitchen. Guess I'm sweeping them before I listen to Dan. Except the trash . . . "Dan! Why are your new shoes in the trash?!"

"I'm telling. A story."

And after multiple requests, he heard me and took his shoes out of the trash. But now I need to clean them.

"You will listen to my story?"

And I want to. But dinner needs to be defrosted and his used-to-be-new shoes are covered with caked disgusting. It's why I've found used dishes in the dirty clothes pile and a toybox stuffed with previously folded jeans.

And I can fix the problems, but I can't make all the things stay straight in Dan's head. And he doesn't want to hear about all those things. Dan just wants to tell his story.

The art Dan makes is full of mad, and maybe I do know why.

Even the Windows Scare Him —

The windowpane is running water-sheets
so that the soggy glass looks fatter now;
it rains so hard the world blurs, and The Dan
was never too connected anyhow.

In rain, the light looks bendy, and Dan thinks
he might be like a window in the rain,
because Dan knows that there's a fence outside,
but it's not looking very fence-y now;
it's just a color without edges. If

The Dan had never seen that fence out there,
it might just be a colored patch of world;
he might not know about the edges, which
explains about mistakes. Dan notices,

but if the world were *always* raining, he
might only see a brown that wiggles. And
Dan doesn't want to think that way again,
'cause thinking like that scares him —

Among Schoolchildren

Dan stared all morning out the window. He ignored me when I tried to engage him. Until he turned to me and started talking. "The windows are weird, in the rain." And it was raining hard, so everything was distorted.

He went on in his somewhat slow and careful way to note that the windows weren't really weird and tomorrow they would look right again. Maybe it was the rain really.

And then in one of his striking pivots — his brain is so much faster than mine in some ways — he asked whether he was the windows or the rain. I'll never be sure, but I think he was asking whether he was the odd thing, the distortion. I told him that he was perfect with his own strengths, and I loved him very much. I meant every word, and he seemed satisfied. I only hope it satisfies him later.

Of Walls and Windows

Dan used to bang his head against the wall
because the wall at least did not pretend
it wasn't there, it wasn't in your way
refusing to be understandable.

In some ways, Dan would like to be a wall,
because a wall is so predictable:
if you want out you look for tunnels, or
(on lucky days) a door. It's people who

are sometimes see-through but you bump them, or
they stand there smudged like windows. Smudges mean
pretend-doors that the cardinals can't see;
Dan saw one smash itself. And honestly

Dan used to be a stupid cardinal
and bang himself on people. But he learned.
And nowadays, when the smudges frustrate him,
he simply picks a wall —

Problems

Even /will admit today was kind of hard. For most of the day I could not figure out why Dan was so overstimulated. He was grumpy too. He would roar at me for misunderstanding even if I was literally repeating his own words back to him.

Joshua kept trying to play with him, but Dan refused to play. He beat his head on the walls and on the sofa. I said the sofa was better. But I could only help him some because now that Dan wouldn't play, I had to spend twice as much time keeping Josh busy. Which got in the way of trying to figure out what was wrong with Dan. Eventually we had to go out to the grocery store. I really didn't want to take the kids out to the store, particularly not like this. But I didn't want to try to serve Dan the Wrong Foods for dinner, not today of all days. Wrong food is hard enough on a good day. And this was the kind of day where I went to the bathroom and when I came out Joshua was beating Dan on the head with his shoe for being in the way. Dan let him because that's who he is. He holds back and doesn't fight until he snaps and decks someone. They call that a really sweet personality or poor self-advocacy, depending on whether they like it or not.

So, I finally got them to the store. It was playing loud music and none of us liked it. Joshua yelled "Too loud!" but instead of turning it down, everyone looked at me and *judged*. Dan shut down in the face of all the noise. And then of course we got the cashier who wanted to pep us all up. I wasn't really that into chatting, so she gave the boys candy, without asking me of course. Well she gave Josh candy. She tried to make Dan smile for her before she'd give him the candy. He wouldn't smile but she kept trying. He banged his head against the cashier's station. The line behind me looked restless, but Dan doesn't smile at strangers. I was trying to get us all out of there. Josh was standing up for Dan though, "But Dan's candy!" when Dan opened his mouth with a big smile. And threw up on her shoes —

And Worse, Breaking Up

It's not just buses now, its grandma. First
the buses break, in long sad painful squeals,
but *nobody* feels sorry for the bus
except for Dan, who clearly doesn't count
because they just ignore him. But it's worse

in grandma's case because she's "breaking up,"
which means her face must be all wiggle-cracks
like puzzle pictures, and Dan knows what's next,
because Josh likes to take the pieces out
when Dan's not looking. But what's worst of all

is that his mom was *smiling*. Dan admits
that smiles can be confusing, but when Dan
explained to Josh that Gran was breaking up,
Josh took a proper outlook on the case
by wailing loudly. And while Dan accepts
that there's a lot of breaking in the world

he can't help liking Grandma, so he hopes
that she at least has glue —

You're Breaking Up

It started when the kids overheard me speaking to Dan's grandmother. As she paced, it became hard to hear. I probably said she was breaking up, something like that.

At any rate, Dan was quite concerned, so I tried to explain. Maybe he picked up on my mood — the phone call was bad news — or probably that was just Dan. Either way, he was sure his grandmother was breaking into pieces. And that got little Joshua going too. "Dan says Grandma is dead!" And that required another explanation. Josh was reassured, but by then we were running so late that the school bus driver had to wait for us or Dan would have never made it.

And I hear there was a bit of an incident on the bus too, which was probably related. Let me give you context first though: We'd been explaining driving recently. "No, we can't drive right now, Josh. The light is red." And more importantly, "Yes, we have to stop for this red light too, Dan. Daddy just braked." And I thought we had sufficiently explained what braking was. But you never know when kids are listening, particularly Dan.

Apparently the bus stopped at a light that had just changed and the brakes squealed a bit. Dan told his aide with increasing emotion that the bus was braking. She agreed, patiently at first and then with bafflement as he eventually had a full meltdown. I suspect he was confusing "breaking" and "braking," but she only says that if he keeps doing this, he can't ride the bus.

Dan Solo

"How are you: *Great!* Dan says he's great. Or not;
you can't say 'no;' that's not an answer. But
a 'not so great' is fine; or you can say
'fine' too *(so many choices).* That's polite —
you can't be wrong, just pick one."

                              Satisfied,
the voice behind the bookcase tries again:

"good boy Dan, thank you! 'Please' and 'thank you,' these
make everybody happy. 'Love you Dan';
what mom says when she hugs you. Just one hug —"
(the bookcase seems to tremble). "Love you mom.
No hugs though: Dan prefers to run away.
She wants one *(poor Mom);* one quick hug? Okay —"

Waking Up

Waking up Dan is when I know I'm doing a good job as a parent He's not particularly a morning person and likes to wake up slowly, with hugs. It's the only time all day I'm allowed to hug him. Later on he might grimly tolerate a hug but usually patting his hair is all I am allowed. But in the mornings he will curl up in my arms. For a few minutes a day, I know how to be intimate with my son.

Then we have to get him dressed and I have to face reality. If we are running early and he is really functional, we might have time to let him dress himself. But that's highly unlikely. Where other five-year-olds dress themselves in seconds and then wait for breakfast, mine curls up into a small ball and says "maaaah" like a goat. If I arrange all his clothes in order, right-side out, he might put them on himself. Usually I have to remind him every minute or so to get back on task. Some days I just give up and dress him.

On the way to school, I remind him how to talk to the world. The crossing guard asks him how he is. She only meant to be kind, but now there's a whole delay in the middle of a busy road as Dan stops to try to decide how he is. "You can say 'fine' or 'great' or . . . Dan turns to her. "No."

On top of that, a passing parent compliments him on his clothes. They only mean to be nice, but it's a whole 'nother hurdle we have to get over. "She complimented you, say 'thank you.' Please and thank you are usually safe words" I suggest. "Please and thank you" Dan says to her.

I post on Facebook about how well Dan is doing. How clever and creative he is. And it's true. He is fantastic. But he doesn't dress himself. He still forgets to use the bathroom when he needs to. Still, don't you dare tell me my son is less functional than others.

Christmas on the Spectrum

It was a stressful morning, so Dan stuffed
a box with pillows and then wedged himself.
Just like a present wrapped in bubble wrap;
a box of Dan. Except that bubble-wrap
explodes when stomped on and Josh does that, so
Dan wrapped himself in *pillows*.

                                    Pillows help,
especially on Christmas morning when
they leapt at him with stockings — *lumpy* ones;

his cereal went soggy on him while
he sorted through the implications. Like
an "ambush" (that is one of Dan's new words).
The floor was crinkly, gift-wrapped —
                                    but the box
was only cardboard, "Dan approved of it"
and although Christmas noises butted in,
he drowned them out with crooning —

Holiday Fun

Most parents don't need to *warn* their sons about Christmas. But I should have warned mine. Some boys would describe a day full of unwrapping gifts and special breakfasts as a treat, a surprise, or fun. Dan called it an ambush. I think it started when I offered bacon and eggs for breakfast instead of cereal. I know he likes bacon and eggs. And to be honest I didn't want to run to the store for cereal on Christmas Eve. But not having cereal, it was an ambush. I finally found a gas station that was open on Christmas and sold cereal. But by the time I had the cereal, he'd been ambushed by stockings until the cereal was soggy and inedible. I made him another bowl of cereal, but I never did get around to eating breakfast.

We opened presents, but even once we turned off the lights and the Christmas music, he found it overstimulating. The wrapping paper was an ambush, and he ignored the new toys. But the box they came in? He climbed right in. Finally, a safe place.

Sorry

Dan's working on it; trust him. There are times
when he can't handle things; he knows that. But
it all stacks up on Dan till he explodes
and mother hates that, so he *sorries* her;
a *string* of sorries ("sorry! Sorry!"), and
she yells, but not at him — Dan always knows

his mother's sorry too. She really tries,
but when it's bad he can't start up again;
he's like a car that way. It's up to her
to find the key to make him run, and then
the words come babbling out; he never means
to make his mother feel bad. And she knows

he's working on it; it's "too much for him;"
he heard his mother say so. But sometimes —
well, "sorry" is the only word he knows.
Dan hopes she's good at listening.

Stupid Effing Chickens

Sometimes it's a mom's job is to be a straight man. He's supposed to be getting dressed, but one tries to be patient. "Hey, guess what, Mom?" Of course, you say what. Even though you know it'll be "chicken butt" yet again. And you may be bored, but you are also proud that Dan is trying to tell jokes like the other kids. You definitely aren't supposed to yell "I know, it's an effing chicken butt, but I'm trying to make you some bloody lunch!"

Obviously, I would never do that. But if one did lose one's temper like that, Dan would certainly apologize. Many times. He turned into a cascade of sorries such as would make a much angrier person feel bad. And then it's even harder to get Dan to get dressed.

Because here it's almost noon and he's *still* half-naked upside down on the sofa. I mean, it's really great that he's found a stim that helps him feel pressure and enjoy it. He's better at life when he goes upside down regularly. But wouldn't it be nice if he could also find the executive function to do a task without three reminders! No, don't say that. Don't even think it. He's doing his best, and he picks up that you wish he did better. Don't give him more guilt. It won't help anything. He needs to express himself and his feelings more. He needs to stand up for himself more.

I've even tried to get him to draw his feelings, to see whether that helped, but all he did was draw question marks. "I'm not dressing, Mom. I'm drawing." They were interesting, strange question marks, but people should dress. And now he's upside down again.

So, patient voice and then the question: "Dan, what shirt do you want to wear"

Behind me, Josh is yelling Guess what! again.

Dan's making eye contact, but no answer.

"Dan!" When I don't answer, Josh fills in "chicken butt." Dan giggles and I lose his attention again.

I put myself into his eye stream. "Buddy, do you want to wear the dinosaur shirt, Batman, or the stupid chicken butts?" I'm not really managing to keep my voice level and peaceful here. And no, Dan doesn't have a chicken shirt, but I'm running out of patience here.

He turned right side up and looked me in the eye. "The stupid chicken butts!"

And we laugh and it's okay, because today he stood up for himself, looked me in the eye, and answered the question. Maybe shirts come later.

Of Birds and Butterflies

The butterflies wear coats now, spangly ones
but only jackets; Dan is worried. Soon
it will be way too cold for butterflies.
If they were only sensible, like birds.
But Dan's been watching, and he's never seen
a double-string of butterflies V-south.

Maybe they wait till evening and *sneak* out.
But butterflies get lost so easily
They'd probably forget and zig-zag north,
or they'd become a *cloud* of butterflies
and get distracted; they can't organize.

A butterfly is an explorer, but
it takes a bird to make an army, and
Dan's noticed that the armies mostly win.
So there may be no butterflies, come spring —

Don't let Dan Bartend

Absolutely no one in my house likes piña coladas except Dan. I mean the kids haven't tasted them, but we all hate them. It started with an ad on Spotify that begins with the famous song. The ad goes on from "piña coladas" to talk about laundry detergent or something. But it comes on a lot and Dan knows those five words. Frustratingly well. Even when the ad is over, he's still singing them over and over. Recently when he sang it, "Do you like piña coladas?" all three voices responded in unison "NOOOOO!"

The problem with living with verbal stims is that they aren't bad. I can't say "don't be repetitive" without being a jerk. I mean, if that's how the kid self-calms, I'd rather have him calm than not. And what if it's "just fun"? Well, I did all kinds of things yesterday for fun. That's valid. But that doesn't make me less bloody sick of piña coladas.

The wiggly stims are "weirder" but actually a lot more awesome. For instance, take his jumps. I can't say Dan likes to jump. Rather, Dan loves to jump. Dan absolutely adores jumping. He jumps holding onto Dad. He jumps holding onto Mom. He jumps on Josh. ("Sorry Joshua.") He jumps while I lift him up. Then he climbs my body and jumps down off my shoulders. He shakes his hands as he jumps alone. Dan broke a trampoline by jumping on it so much.

Lately Dan has a new one though; he waves his arms like a bird. Though I can hear him correcting me now. "No. Mom, I am a butterfly."

Or just yesterday "I'm a butterfly. I'm cold!" I offered him a coat, but he was insulted. Said something about butterflies only wearing jackets. But he didn't want to wear a jacket either. Instead he did one of his confusing topic changes and said he was going to fight an army. I guess his conversational skills need some work too. But the way Dan flaps and jumps around . . . Let's be honest, no one thought Dan was "normal" anyway. Forget normal, he's Dan, and that's how we all love him anyway. Keep on being a cold butterfly son. Just don't ask me about the piña coladas.

Of Meteor-Rights and other Evils

A meteor-right killed the dinosaurs,
but Dan refuses to believe that since
two meteor-wrongs never make a right,
and Dan is missing out on dinosaurs
'cause *that* one couldn't aim. But Mom just laughed

without explaining, so the Dan was cross,
and had long conversations with himself,
because he likes the way Dan listens. Till

there was an interruption about chairs.
Between the rude, erratic meteors
and the upsetting lack of dinosaurs,
Dan didn't have a lot of space for chairs.

He scurried over though, obediently.
He even asked her (being logical)
if he should *sit* instead of standing there,
though she forgot to say so. Then instead
she rudely called Dan "Smart-ass . . ."

Socks and Bears

Dan put on bears today. And *ate* his bears. And after that, he even *brushed* his bears. He isn't usually interested in bears —

But anyone gets tired of the morning grind. Particularly when people make so little sense. Even the easy things were hard today. Josh asked me for a real dinosaur, so I explained about extinct. And that of all things was a trigger for Dan. I get that the boys wish dinosaurs were still real, but when I said the dinosaurs had been killed by a meteorite, Dan erupted. "WRONG! A meteor WRONG WRONG WRONG!" He ran to the couch, and Josh began to cry.

The neighbors complained of noise again, and Dan's father doesn't understand why I can't keep the children quiet.

That whole conversation was already putting us at risk of being late for school and pre-school. But I don't blame Dan for being tired of confusing bossy adults. So today I said "Please put your socks . . ."

"Bears bears bears!"

"Okay, please put your socks and bears on."

And then he laughs and you know there's one fight you won't have to have today. Because laughter isn't screaming.

Metaphorical Ducks

Dan's quacking for the ducks that Mom can't see;
he knows because he asked her. And he's loud,
but that's because they're very *noisy* ducks;
it's hard to focus on her questions when
the ducks keep interrupting. Even when

she grabs his head, and it's quite interesting
the way her mouth moves — they're such *plaintive* ducks,
they sound like grandma on the telephone,
a sputtering. So Dan makes up the words
until "— you haven't answered." He heard that,
and "yes, you haven't" he agrees with her;

but yes, it didn't help. His face is trapped,
and there's a lot of ways of seeing ducks,
but Dan has one too many —

The Dangers of Driving to Grandma's

If you will forgive me for mentioning myself — I'm "Mom," things aren't supposed to be about me — it was plants that helped me know why Dan hates bathrooms. It happens I am allergic to some common lawn spray. Guess I'm a weed. It feels as if the air is poison ivy, seeping in. It attacks me from all sides and it's scary because you never know when it's going to hit.

And I think that might be how Dan feels in public bathrooms. You wouldn't, on the face of it, consider him a terrible person to take on a road trip. In the car mostly he thinks, almost never complains. But sometimes he needs to pee. And public bathrooms have hand driers. Hand driers are funnels that point huge amounts of noise right at small boys' ears; unpleasant for anyone, but holy hell for Dan. Sometimes fear of hair driers will make Dan not pee for a whole day on the road. Imagine if the very air of all bathrooms were dormant poison ivy, quiet for now but ready. Ready to turn your whole world into a violent painful attack you couldn't run away from. If I ever coax poor Dan into a bathroom, we hurry as much as we can to get him out to safety. When I hear a woman enter the bathroom I tremble. If she's faster than Dan . . . He pulls his pants up, but young hands are clumsy. She's opened the stall. He's doing his zipper. She washes her hands, but he's got his pants buttoned. Dan rushes out of the stall. Maybe we'll make it? I run with Dan — we'll clean his hands in the car with wipes — just in time for the air to blast my son to smithereens.

She looks at us in puzzlement. "Kids these days!"

And for hours afterward Dan is so easily overwhelmed. If Josh sings in the car, Dan quacks. If a police car goes noisily by, Dan quacks. If the radio gets too excitable, of course Dan quacks. In fact, when I ask Dan what he wants to eat for lunch, I get nothing more than quacks or confusing agreements that he has not answered me. Bathrooms are hard, and yet they blame the kids.

Forks

Dan uses forks now. He prefers a spoon
because a scoop is easier, but forks
are just expected, so he had to learn
to *stab* his macaroni. He's concerned
about the ice-cream though, where stabs don't work
although it's fun to try, and pretty soon
there isn't any, which distresses him.

He shouldn't have to poke bananas though,
or strawberries; that is *outrageous*. But
she must have had a lot of leftovers
and cut them up to make it hard for him.
So Dan decided cheese was safer, and
he asked *politely;* please and thank you. But
she wouldn't listen; it was forks today —

What's For Lunch?

Dan had a fruit salad today and I considered that a major success on my part. No, not because it's hard to get Dan to eat fruit. He's fine about fruit. Today, after we got back from seeing ducks at the lake, we were all hungry and tired. Dan wanted a grilled cheese sandwich. But there isn't any bread until I can go to the store, maybe this afternoon. I made Josh some mac and cheese, but Dan was not even slightly interested. "No thanks. I want a grilled cheese sandwich."

At first we made some progress. When I suggested he start with fruit, he said "Give me a banana."

I told him to ask politely, but Dan always struggles with formal speech. He froze up. Joshua suggested he "Say please, Dan!"

And poor Dan cooperates "Please Dan." And I'm afraid I didn't hide my amusement. Joshua giggled for sure. Dan turned pink and ran away. After that, he definitely did not want a banana! Once I finally got him to talk at all, he wanted nothing but his grilled cheese sandwich.

And no matter what else I offered him, I got that answer. "No thanks. I want a grilled cheese sandwich." Every time I asked him something, he looked more stressed. But hunger is stressful too. If I didn't feed him soon, I knew he would go boom. By now I was pretty tired and hungry, and I had no idea what to feed my stubborn oldest son. I got out my own planned lunch, a Greek salad with tomatoes and feta and what not.

"Is that a fruit salad?" Dan asks. I thought about it and the cliché about tomatoes being fruits but not belonging in a fruit salad. And I knew my son wanted a fruit salad, but I didn't want to lie.

"Well, it's a tomato salad."

"But is it a fruit salad?"

I said I guessed so as tomatoes were fruit and tucked the cucumber under the tomatoes. I did warn him it wasn't sweet, but he said he'd take it, if it was a fruit salad.

Now I just have to figure out what *I'll* eat.

Busy Being Dan

I'm busy being *Dan,* Mom. There are ducks
parading in Dan's head, so Joshua
can be a line of ducklings. Joshua
is smaller, so he has to let Dan pick,

but Dan lets him pretend. And here's the fort
for ducks that Dan made. Josh said, "Can I see?"
"Good asking, Josh," Dan said supportively
because big brothers say that — but he's short,

so no, he couldn't. And when he climbed out
Dan said Josh was a duck, and ducks stay put.
Mom, there are cheetahs out there. This can't be
about what ducks want; not in cat country.

Josh makes a good duck; he goes everywhere.
But ducks aren't good at holding an idea —

Tea with the Ducks

Morning tea with the kids on a Saturday is wonderful. I will admit it sometimes tries my patience. All that quacking! The boys are noisy creatures too. It comes with the age. But Dan's patience with repeated noises is his and only his.

Of course, I couldn't even get my tea until I got the boys' breakfast. Josh asked for cereal. Dan quacked, and asked for his medium glass bowl, which is actually plastic. I asked whether he wanted raisin bran too.

"Quack! Quack, QUACK, QUACK, QUACK!"

I shrugged and tried to get my tea. There was suddenly a medium plastic bowl pushed at me.

"Mooom! Quack, quack, quack!" I sighed. At least I got the kettle filled this time.

"Dan, do you want raisin bran or toasty o's?"

"Quack, quack, quack, QuAAACK!"

"Dan! You are not listening!" His face fell when I said that. I had upset him. But no answer except quacking.

I tried a few more times but with no better result. I showed him the boxes too. Sometimes when Dan's not verbal, pointing still works. But he was mightily distracted, so nothing but the infernal ducks. Eventually I gave up and got him the toasty o's.

"Ah!" I said to myself. "The tea should be ready about now." But when I checked, I'd never turned the kettle on. So hard to keep one's head straight while parenting. I barely fixed my oversight before it turned out that Dan did not want toasty o's and was now eating Joshua's abandoned raisin bran to Josh's extreme fury. Josh screamed and hit Dan. Dan kept eating.

Before I had that one worked out — I'd eat the bloody toasty o's with my tea, if I could ever get it — the tea kettle was whistling. Dan covered his ears and ran out of the room looking very upset. But Josh went back to eating his raisin bran, so I headed to finally get the kettle. My tea even finished steeping before I heard Josh yelling again.

I wistfully put my tea down, undrunk, and went to their room. Dan had created a large blanket fort with all my sofa cushions and half our blankets. (I know who would be cleaning that up!) Josh was in the fort. Good to see them playing together.

"No, Josh, you are a duck. You have to stay in."

"I WANNA GO!"

"I'm sorry Josh but you have to stay. It's not safe out there."

At this point, before I could intervene, Joshua tried to push his way out. The blanket fort, inevitably, fell in on him, about when Dan proclaimed that if Josh left, he would be eaten by cheetahs. Joshua started crying, something incomprehensible about the blanket fort and the cheetahs.

I have a feeling I know where Josh gets those nightmares about being eaten by cats now. Of course, by the time I had comforted him the cereal was soggy and the tea cold.

Grimms Fairy Tales

Dan has discovered changelings, and suspects
that if he ever met the evil Grimm
Dan would have danced, and been denounced by him
as yet another bogus baby. Dan
has no idea what's wrong with dancing, but

he does his best to keep his wiggles in,
because when sneaky people see him stim
they think he's a replacement, subbing in
for someone placid, someone more like *them*.

Dan tries to fit, but it's discouraging
to think he's actually an alien.
It could be worse though. Because now and then

he thinks about the way it must have been
in fairyland, for that poor other-him,
an ordinary baby —

Who's Bad?

I collect sea glass. It's an excuse to get out to the Lake. It's best in the cold weather because the only other people are also seeking quiet. The waves come in and out and there is nothing you should be doing.

Sometimes I take a child or walk with another grownup, but I try not to take more than one person, if I take anyone. Today I came with Dan. We walk hand in hand, and we don't need words. Besides, it's been a hard day. Josh is visiting a friend, and I read Dan a story for just-us time. It was a classic fairy tale with an evil spirit who dances to cast spells. We were enjoying it until Dan burst into tears. He said *he* was the bad guy and he didn't *want* to be poofed away. "But I can't stop dancing!" Even as he said it, his fingers were stimming.

I told him that his dances didn't make people do things they didn't want to do, and that solved the problem temporarily. So, we have come out here where the water moves more repetitively than anyone. For now, I am collecting sea glass, but I can't stay here forever.

Dan Needs a Question-Swatter

Dan doesn't go in order; he can't make
a list, his head's too bouncy. So to him
it's like mosquitoes when they question him.

He offers them the stories in his head,
But that excites them. Yet not answering
(which is his favorite way of handling them)
just makes more questions; you can flail at them,
but they come back with friends.

                              Still, now and then
he tells a story they can recognize,
which means they give him space to breathe in. And
Dan isn't stupid; he can memorize.

So now when people ask about his day
he talks of bells and lunch and chocolate milk,
because that always happens. And Dan thinks

that if *they* ask the same old questions, he
can give the same old answers —

Talking to Dan

I swear, people make Dan itch. Not literally, but whenever people get too social, he backs away: It's as if he can only bear so much human interaction. Sometimes he says that people buzz. Still, conversation is an art the lad needs just to function in this world. So, every day I ask about his school day. I used to ask open-ended questions: "How was your day?" "What did you learn at school?" "What did you do?"

But Dan never answers those questions. So, I moved to yes or no questions. "Did you have fun?" "Did you play with kids?" "Did you learn something?" And sometimes I can follow up with asking what was fun, who he played with, and so forth. At least those are more directed open-ended questions. And I ask the same few questions so that he will get used to them. Before he gets on the bus, I tell him which question I will ask when he gets home. But every day I hear that Dan had played with kids at lunch, he had fun drinking chocolate milk, and he heard bells. In short, there's definitely room for improvement.

On the other hand, Dan's father never could stay in a room full of talking people either. Makes it hard to go to parties. He always stayed on the side or eventually sidled away. When people itch, and questions bite, well, a kid needs his space.

Dan Has At Least One Friend

"Ask nicely" she says, and the whole world stares
at Dan, who doesn't want it anymore;
of course he freezes. Then to make it worse
the duckling Joshua, whom Dan protects,
decides to help, and elbows him: "please, Dan —"

But Dan feels pressured, so he says "please Dan,"
and everybody laughs, and Dan forgets
whatever he decided not to want,
but Joshua won't stop helping. "No, say please!"
but now it sounds like quacking, so Dan quacks

exactly like him till Josh takes his hand
and she gives up and offers something but
The Dan can't see it so Josh takes it, and
they go away together —

Dan's Best Friend

Dan has a best friend now, he says. Though it certainly isn't like how I act with my best friends. We don't sit on far ends of the sofa, pressed carefully into the corners to be as far away from each other as we can. And if we did sit that way, we certainly wouldn't then ignore each other! Of course, anyone who can't talk won't qualify to be my best friend. But I'm trying to be open minded here. And at least this friendship isn't all in his mind; Luna really does particularly like Dan. And she is a very good dog.

But I worry about the lad and wish he had more human friends. He's happy enough with Josh, and Josh is even trying to help us teach Dan social words. We generally accept that Dan currently interchanges *please* and *thank you,* but Josh has a mission. "Thank you is not how you ask nicely!" Josh encourages him to socialize with other kids too. Josh explained to Dan the other day that learning his classmates' names would help with making friends.

But even when he does know the names, Dan doesn't quite understand socialization yet.

If he answers a question like "Did you do anything with any kids?" I get told about Ronnie or Nazeem, but if I ask what he did with Nazeem? I get "Good." I wonder if Nazeem has noticed Dan at all. I'm pretty sure they don't exactly play together, but maybe they at least play nearby? I could picture two sweet boys playing next to each other happily. And if that's good enough for Dan and Nazeem? I guess it's good enough for me. Or it better be.

Dan the Dragon Killer

The blow-dryer was yelling at him, and
it isn't fair to yell at Dan like that.
Noise squatted on him till the claws dug in;
"Take the Despair off, please!" but no one did
though to be fair Josh tried. Dan thinks the roar
turned Joshua into a dinosaur —
and then Dan squashed him.

                                       But he *had* to. Like
he squashed the vacuum, which was bigger than
both Dan and Josh together, and it roared
like *three* despairs until Dan mashed the prongs.
Most people just suspected it was Josh.
Which makes Dan feel bad, but the way cords shriek
He has to interrupt, and Josh won't speak.
There must be somebody to blame it on —

Drowning in Emotion

I tell people the boys are best of friends. But even best friends fight. Today was that sort of day. Dan is pretty easy going, but there are so many things he can't control. Adult rules come in waves, and the poor kid can't fight them, so he *needs* to control the bits of life that are left. Then Josh comes along with opinions. Little brothers are supposed to cooperate, particularly when big brother really does know better. If instead little brother insists on ruining the project? There will be tears.

And this wasn't just tears. This was a full-fledged meltdown, the autism word for when there's no control. Past a certain point, control just isn't possible. All Dan can do is fall as the waves break over him.

So when Joshua left for a playdate, Dan and I went to the beach for quiet. It was too cold for most people, so the sand was quiet. We walked to the end of the pier, surrounded by water. If you focus on the water, it seems as if the whole world is flowing. When a big wave comes, I find myself stepping back to avoid it even though I know it can't touch us. The waves flow, and I try to explain. "Waves are irresistible. When they come, sometimes you have to let them break over you."

Dan takes over. "But then the waves are broken."

"Exactly. That's the thing about waves. After they break, you will still be there."

If Only the Heads Stayed On —

Dan's Lego-people need a hospital
because he drops them, and their heads fall off.
Or else they're sitting on their vehicles
and hit a bump, and then they're down to stumps
in bright-red pants, a stubborn bottom half
perched, resolute as always. Joshua says
that hospitals can put the heads back on,
but first you have to *find* them — and Dan tries,

but Joshua gets bored and wanders. If
the pegs fit better, or we found the girl
before the radiator melted her,
we wouldn't be so short of people. We
have legs left, and a pair of overalls.
But somebody should teach them how to fall —

Listening

Dan hates when his World isn't tidy. And I don't mean he's neat. Rather the opposite really; The lad lives in his Giant World, so he often doesn't notice physical mess. But Dan hates when thoughts aren't tidied off. And a Lego person with no head is absolutely not okay. Josh suggested the hospital could put a cylinder piece on for a head. But Dan was not impressed. "I need. The head!"

He and Josh were playing this morning and Josh got bored. There were too many delays for headless Lego figures, and he is still young. "But we need to finish the game! Josh! We have to finish the game. So, we will be able to play it again, later."

It felt like an echo of his father years ago "Not finishing feels like dying." Maybe if I could have understood that years ago, things would have gone differently. But I'm like Josh, and sometimes it's time to stop. I found the boys a way to shift their game so that Dan could finish up his Lego people driving Lego cars while Josh played train tracks. We live in a commuter world, just drop off your car at the train station, guys. Everyone rides the train these days, even the headless people. They were both too young to understand what their brother needed, so I played diplomat.

Sometimes you can't fix the past, so you fix the present. I'm learning to talk to my son the way his father and I never learned to talk. But no. I am learning to listen to my son the way his father and I should have listened.

And maybe that's part of the problem; the boys feel their life is short of people, not just Legos. Dan's father moved out, and he won't be coming back. They still see him, but there are fewer hands to help around the house, and fewer parents here. But there are fewer fights too. He and I couldn't make it work, but with the boys it will be different. We will learn how to listen — and to fall.

Questions Only Come in Black and White —

Dan's head is full of colored answers, but
the questions only come in black and white,
so when Dan tries to squeeze the meaning out
his voice goes gray like pencils. In his head

his voice goes up and down like music, but
a secret monster sucks the color out
till nothing's left but bones, and they get stuck;
Dan has to take a breath and shove them out
to talk at all, and Dan can hear himself:

words flat and colorless with gaps inside,
because Dan has to stop and concentrate.
If he could tell you with his *inside* voice
and you could see his bouncing colors, then

we'd talk about a hundred things at once
exactly as they happen, and not fuss.
If they could only hear his *inside* voice —

What Do You Like?

Today in digital pandemic school Dan's class was told to share something they liked. "If you can, write a sentence. If you can't, write a word, or tell us what you like." And then his teacher gave an example. She gave a couple examples, rather wordy. Maybe she just gave Dan too much time to think. Either way he started off with his imaginary character Tiny Chris the Mouse in Mile Function. (I'm pretty sure Mile function is a mispronunciation of Malfunction since the original story was about a tech malfunction, but Dan says otherwise.) I agreed that Tiny Chris was absolutely likable. But his teacher was still talking, so he kept thinking. He started to draw out a whole story.

"Dan, write what you like."

"I'm. Not. Done."

As he drew, he narrated, and the story got more complicated.

"Dan, it's a great story, but you should write what you like."

He just looked at me, and I knew there was no way he could write that story. There wasn't enough time left for *me* to write that story, let alone him.

He buried his head in his hands, and it was still there when his teacher called on him. Finally, he held up his picture.

"Dan, you were supposed to write something you liked. Did you pay attention?

He put his head back down.

But the computer went on talking. "Dan! Can you tell me something you like?"

"Dan, well tell me. Do you like TV?"

Finally, Dan raised his head and responded in monotone. "I. like. TV."

Manifesto

Dan types himself: three letters. But the screen
is positive that Dan is not a word,
so it decides that what he really means
is "dandelion." Well, he *doesn't*. Dan
is not a puff-ball; you can't scatter him
and leave a naked-headed stemmy thing
like leg-less daddy longlegs. And he's not

a typo either; somebody's mistake
you can go back and fix. Dan *knows* himself.
So when he says he's meant to be like this —
well, people should believe him, but they don't;
they're just like the computer. On the screen
it's possible to back-space, so Dan does.
But in the real-world Dan's just somebody
who can't be left alone —

Self Confidence

I'm pretty sure I know what Dan's teacher did *not* expect for her Thanksgiving question: "Dan is good. Dan is thankful for Dan."

But I was very proud of that answer. Yes, he can talk, and if you help him spell the words, he can write. But even his spoken words don't nearly touch his depths, and his writing is a puddle compared to what he has to say. All his life Dan's been told he didn't fit. He did things wrong. He should do it like everyone else. So if Dan knows that Dan is good, if Dan is thankful for Dan? I'm thrilled.

Today pandemic school was hard. Dan's one of the "smart" kids because he is verbal. He even has the hand control and executive function to write. It's all about co-morbid conditions. Autism doesn't cause bad hand control, but many people with autism have other conditions too and Dan has "poor muscle tone." He could have it much worse. Some of his classmates need tools to speak, but Dan can be expected to write sentences. He puts in the effort and writes those sentences very well. Dan's handwriting is downright beautiful. I think his teacher figures he is slow because he draws so much. In truth, I think he draws to deal with the frustration of hand control. "When I write or type . . . nothing comes out right!"

What she doesn't see is how hard he works to write that way. He does not write quickly, not as quickly as they expect. But Dan's writing is better than mine. Better than yours too. Not only are there are no backwards letters, there are no lines out of place. And of course he uses proper punctuation, perfect spelling.

They have computer programs that they think would help Dan. They suggested he might get his ideas down faster if he used a word processing program sometimes. But Dan won't use them. He says the computer doesn't know what words are. I don't blame him though. He simply wants to write it down his way.

Today I had to pull Dan off his computer and let him stop writing his sentences because the class went on without him. I'm sure they figured he should be done by now. They figured he was goofing off. Why did his paper still say "Europeans came to Ameri"? When I pulled him off, Dan left and got three pieces of paper. Each paper said "Dan is good." He had to erase the good a few times because it kept wanting to say dooG, but he got it right.

Dan writes better than anyone else in his class. Do they know how much it costs him?

Fist of Doom

Dan's not allowed to use the Fist of Doom
for pens, but when he holds it tight that way,
the pen feels safer. If you give it room
it wiggles anxiously and disobeys;

it wants a hug. So Dan makes a cocoon
out of his fingers, but that's not allowed.
They pry his fingers open, "showing" him,
and now the pen feels naked. Dan sits bowed

and waits until their shadows go away,
but then he *fists* it (warm safe happy pen)
and makes his letters large and wobbly, loud
as Dan would like to be. No, none of them

stay in the lines; the pen refuses. And
it feels a lot like Dan —

Writing

Handwriting hasn't been going well. Dan will never have the best hand control. They have a word for it, but what they meant was 'Bad handwriting is the best Dan can ever hope for, if he practices. So we work on it. But handwriting's a bear even when you're not naturally terrible at it. So, he hides in the bathroom, again.

He doesn't answer even when I put it as a knockknock joke:

> "Dan, knockknock."
> "Who's there?"
> "Why?"
> "Why won't the boy come out of the bathroom?"

But maybe that's the wrong question. Maybe I should really be asking why does the boy go into the bathroom? It's certainly not for the usual reasons. People doing their business don't run laps back and forth back and forth. People doing their business don't slam into the door repeatedly.

With Dan, figuring out why often involves thinking about what happened right before. Well, right before he hid in the bathroom, came the damn handwriting practice. Dan's teacher — digitally because pandemic — reminded him to hold the pen properly. He isn't supposed to hold it like a fist. So, I gently showed him how to put his hands. Immediately he had to use the bathroom, and I think he brought the pen with him. In the bathroom, no one tells you how to write. Maybe the question I should really be asking is why have we built a world where Dan is only free in the bathroom?

Accident

Dan's feet are in the bathroom, and his head
can pay attention when it wants to, but
he left it on the Red-Line. At the end
there is a car with buttons Dan can drive
that makes the train go backwards; it's pretend,
but Dan enjoys pretending *('pants down')*. Dan's
not interested in pants-down. But he does
need buttons, so he finds one *("good job Dan")*
although it's slow since drivers can't look down;
his hands get no instruction. And because
trains talk a lot *("Doors Open on the Right")*
its hard to pay attention to the voice
that's in the bathroom; it said closer but
("Doors Closing; please don't lean against the doors")
Dan doesn't dare. And now his feet are wet —

Executive Function

At least I found Dan's new shirt when it was in the trash today. It isn't that he meant to throw it away, you understand. It's just that a trash can is like a laundry bin and a closet as a place where you get rid of things. We've found his shoes in the dirty laundry too, and his underwear is sometimes in the closet.

It used to be that we knew whenever Dan struggled. They called that "he can't mask." But he's growing and trying to become "normal" and the person he thinks we want him to be. So now there are the days when we think he's doing great. Right up until something as simple as setting the table reduces him to tears of shame. Too hard. And of course, he can't explain exactly what is the matter. One moment he walks to the dishwasher and then suddenly it's all too much and he's crying on the sofa.

Careful now, if you say the wrong thing, he'll run for further quiet, to his bed. And he'll be even more frantic then. So I'm quiet, just waiting. No eye contact, that can be a trigger. Don't say his name either. Just gently, "Did something . . ."

"NOOOOOO"

Okay, so don't, even gently.

At least he's getting better at self-calming. Because he shut himself in the bathroom — uhoh — but soon after I started hearing "good job Dan" and something about leaning on the door. It was in his train driver voice, so I think he's in his imaginary world.

When he came out, he told me that the dishwasher was too full, and it poked at him. I'm guessing that there were so many things in the dishwasher he couldn't figure out what he needed. I told him it was fine anyway. Now if I could just stop worrying —

And does anyone know why Dan's pants are wet?

Doing His Best

It came out wrong, Dan fears it. He was tired
but order matters — which means naked first;
she needs to stop forgetting. She may *like*
his dinosaur pajamas; so does Dan.
But they get stuck on street-pants, and what's worse
he had no feet left, and the words were gone
and it got very noisy —

                  Naked first.
Then she said "toothbrush" and escaped again,
which meant Dan had to climb to reach it, and
there was a lot of blue paste, but it worked
so well, he brushed tyrannosauri too,
because their mouths are always open. So
she should have told him he was *"organized!"*
when she came back, because she likes that word
and Dan deserved it. But she only found
the train pajamas, and began again.

It was a very tiring bedtime —

Dinosaurs

Inside Dan there are two dinosaurs . . . And no this isn't the old cliché about wolves. This one Dan told me himself. One dinosaur talks. It seems a somewhat normal human-type dinosaur.

"The other dinosaur only roars. Except when it is in the special cave. And then it does talk, but it's very strange."

"I like strange, Dan."

"Me too." And he said it cheerfully, which comforts me because I see a metaphor here. And then I stop because he's talking again. "I think the dinosaurs are me, if I were a dinosaur." So then I know he sees the metaphor too.

I love both dinosaurs equally, but one of them is definitely better at schoolwork than the other. And when I ask Dan to put his trains away, if the non-talking dinosaur is supreme, he will need to be reminded about every train track. If I'm there, it helps. My very existence is sometimes enough reminder to get the trains put away. But my existence is a distraction too.

It's all about how you put things. I tried to tell Dan's grandma about the two dinosaurs, but I used the wrong phrase, so Dan was mad. His correction meant exactly the same thing to me, but to him the difference was essential. I think it doesn't take much to derail the quiet dinosaur. Still, I can't afford to let people turn Dan into just a 'normal' dinosaur. Because then I'd lose half my boy. And the strange half is really my favorite half.

Epilogue: Someday —

Dan at 50

The universe may well be breakable,
but words bounce off, and Dan's not writing this,
for magpies dance derision on the roof
and Dan's not in the mood for listening
to those sarcastic magpies — this is Dan
with grown-up words and mixed-up politics,
whose figments don't pan out.

                      But there are Dans
who pick up water-bottles in the sand
so that the ocean doesn't choke itself:
whose universes stick together. And

he can imagine leggy, bearded Dans
who scamper with the run-and-scurry birds
that live on foam and seaweed, in the verge
between the scrabble-earth of stupid men,
and whales who never touch us. And he hopes

that those of you who have become his friends
will be so lucky and will run with him.
And we will laugh together —

Acknowledgements

"Behind the Bookcase" appeared in *Tiny Tim Literary Review,* Summer 2, 2017.

"Dan Hates Holidays," appeared in *Snakeskin* 231 July 2016 (retitled and revised, Christmas on the Spectrum).

"Dan Solo," appeared in *From Sac*, IV, Outsiders Issue, Nov. 2016.

"Busy Being Dan" appeared in *Better Than Starbucks* March 2018.

About the Authors

Kathryn Jacobs is a nomad who travels about the country in an RV, writing poetry and editing the metrical poetry journal *The Road Not Taken*. A retired professor, she is almost certainly on the spectrum, and likes it like that. In her former life she was a medievalist at Texas A&M-C.

Along the way she wore various hats, as most of us do sooner or later. In her youth she took a masters from the University of Michigan and a doctorate from Harvard, after which she published a scholarly book with the University Press of Florida called *Marriage Contracts From Chaucer to the Renaissance Stage*. As time passed, however, poetry took up more and more of her attention, as witness the hundreds of poems she published in a variety of poetry journals, from *Measure* and *New Formalist* to *Mezzo Cammin* and *Whiskey Island, Third Wednesday, Wordgathering,* and *Better Than Starbucks*. She also published five solo volumes of poetry: *Advice Column and Signs and Portents* (Finishing Line Press), *to Signs of Our Time* (Pudding House Press), *In Transit* (David Roberts Press) and *Wedged Elephant* (Kelsay Books).

Finally, and in between all that, she married, divorced, remarried, had three children, and lost one (Raymond Jacobs, 18).
Life is what you make of it —

Rachel Jacobs lives in Chicago proper with one husband, three kids, one sister, two dogs, and one cat. Some of the housemates are autistic, but the pets are probably not. In between having a family and writing for fun, they have a fulltime job editing proposals.

Rachel spent almost 20 years writing and editing textbooks. They started off with a post college job at McGraw Hill, lost it in the Great Recession, and then managed to support three children as a freelance editor for the intervening years. Recently Rachel gave up on educational publishing and moved to the government services industry.